THE GOSPEL IS...

Cole Brown

Copyright © 2016 Cole Brown
All rights reserved.

All rights reserved. No part of this publication may be reproduced, distributed, or transmitted in any form or by any means, including photocopying, recording, or other electronic or mechanical methods, without the prior written permission of the publisher, except in the case of brief quotations embodied in critical reviews and certain other noncommercial uses permitted by copyright law. For permission requests, write to the publisher, addressed "Attention: Permissions Coordinator", at the email below.

Special discounts are available on quantity purchases by corporations, associations, ministries and others. For details, contact the publisher at hola@colebrown.es.

Scriptures taken from the Holy Bible, New International Version®, NIV®. Copyright © 1973, 1978, 1984, 2011 by Biblica, Inc.™ Used by permission of Zondervan. All rights reserved worldwide. www.zondervan.com The "NIV" and "New International Version" are trademarks registered in the United States Patent and Trademark Office by Biblica, Inc.™

Dedicated to every member of every church I have been a part of, each of whom has helped contribute to removing the gospel from the realm of theory and bringing it to the most profound parts of my heart and life.

TABLE OF CONTENTS

Author's Note	i
A Note to Leaders	iii

INTRODUCTION	1
Discussion Guide 5	
…NOT WHAT WE OFTEN THINK	11
Discussion Guide 16	
…THE GOOD NEWS…	19
Discussion Guide 23	
…OF WHO JESUS IS…	27
Discussion Guide 33	
…AND WHAT JESUS HAS DONE…	36
Discussion Guide 42	
…FOR THE GLORY OF GOD…	45
Discussion Guide 49	
…AND FOR THE GOOD OF GOD'S PEOPLE.	51
Discussion Guide 57	
NOW WHAT?	51
Discussion Guide	

Bible Passages for Further Study

AUTHOR'S NOTE

Thank you for picking up *The Gospel Is:* I wrote this book after planting a church in my home city of Portland, pastoring it for 9 years, and then moving to Mexico City, Mexico to help plant another church. In my ministry experience in both places, I learned over and over again that what we Christians call "the gospel" is not only the most important message in the history of the world, but also the most misunderstood. I wrote this book in the hope that it might cut through the muddy misunderstandings and provide both Christians and non-Christians alike a simple, easy-to-follow summary of the Bible's main message. You, as the listener, will be the judge of whether or not it succeeds in doing so.

In order to make the summary as direct and easy-to-listen to as possible we have not included scripture references in the body of the book. Instead, we have provided an appendix of relevant Bible passages at the end of the book, which we will hope you will use to verify my claims and grow more in your understanding of the gospel.

In my time in ministry, I have also learned that truth is best discovered in the context of community. For this reason, we wanted to make it as easy as possible for you to work through this content with a small group of people who are also interested in this topic. At the close of each chapter, you will find a discussion guide that you can use to provoke discussion and prayer with others as you take a fresh look at the most powerful message in history.

If you do plan on working through *The Gospel Is:* in a group, be sure to read "A Note to Leaders" on the next page, which explains how the discussion guide is designed and how you can make the most of it with your group.

Whether you choose to listen to this book on your own or within the context of community, we want you to know that we have prayed for you. May you see the gospel in such a way that your heart is both captured and transformed.

With hope,

Cole Brown

A NOTE TO LEADERS: BEFORE YOU BEGIN

Thank you for choosing to lead a discussion group on *The Gospel Is:*. It is our hope that the 8 weeks you spend working through this material will prove to be much more than just a discussion. We believe God can and will use this group to clarify the core message of the Bible and help you apply this life-transforming message to your daily life. Please take the time to read this "note to leaders" in its entirety before beginning your group.

With the exception of the first week, which includes a general introduction to the study, the guide for each week is broken into three sections designed to last around one hour in total.

1) Chapter Summary (3-5 minutes). This provides a brief summary of the main point of each week's assigned chapter. It's there to help keep you and the group focused on the main objective of each week, which is to understand apply the truths taught in the chapter. You may find it helpful to read this summary at the beginning of each session or to have others summarize the week's listening in their own words.

2) Discussion Questions (40 minutes). This is the heart of why your group is gathering: to process the truths of the book and their implications in the context of a supportive

Christian community. The questions are designed to help each participant connect the truths of the gospel to his or her heart so that the message will not only be clarified, but also stick.

3) <u>Prayer (10-15 minutes)</u>. As we reflect on the message of God's gospel, our hearts should be moved toward prayer—prayers of gratitude and thanksgiving, prayers for greater understanding, prayers for opportunities to share the message with others, and more. This is why we encourage you to set aside 10-15 minutes for group prayer at the end of each session. This is not intended to be a time when you as the leader pray a quick prayer on behalf of everyone. This is why we also provide guidelines to help you and your group pray for the issues at hand, though we also encourage you to follow the Holy Spirit and pray as he leads.

In order to help you succeed, we recommend that your group follow four simple ground rules. Be sure to establish these expectations clearly during the opening minutes of your first meeting, and briefly remind the group about them at the start of each subsequent meeting:

1. <u>Confidentiality</u>. What is shared in this group is for the members of this group alone. At times people will share details of personal experiences or struggles that they might be hesitant to speak about otherwise. It is essential, then, that your group knows that

they can do so without fear of what they share being delivered to others outside of the group.

As the leader, you must model this if you expect people to follow this.

2) <u>Authority</u>. In any book discussion, everyone has an opinion on the topic at hand, including the author. While the book should be used as the guide to the themes you are discussing, you should emphasize that the authority on what the gospel is does not rest in Cole Brown, or in you, or in the members of the group—it rests in the Scriptures. For this reason, we have intentionally included multiple passages from Scripture for you to read and discuss in each session.

As the leader, this starts with you. Be sure your group devotes adequate time to examining the Scriptures in each section and that they understand that there is a difference between the authority of the words of this book and the authority of the words of The Book. Model this by using the Bible passages to reinforce or improve upon what is written in the book.

3) <u>Consistency</u>. Group members are expected to faithfully attend all eight meetings, faithfully listen to the book, and regularly participate in the discussion. If members display inconsistency, though, do not write them off; instead, use this as an opportunity to help them examine their heart. What are they running from? What are they hiding from? Are

they truly interested in understanding the core message Jesus preached? Or is it simply an issue of life circumstances conflicting with their group participation? If so, can the group help to alleviate those circumstances in any way?

As the leader, you help create this culture by always being on time and always being prepared.

4) <u>Resist the Temptation to Do More</u>. *The Gospel Is:* is intentionally short and simple. Each chapter should only take around 10 minutes to listen to. For this reason, your group might be interested in listening to multiple chapters or discussing multiple chapters each week. We strongly encourage you to resist this temptation. We believe that the simple message of the gospel shows itself to be much more profound in focused group discussion. If you listen to more chapters or try to cover more ground in a single meeting, you will minimize the time available for highly focused discussion and highly focused prayer. More can be accomplished in eight weeks of highly focused meetings than in fewer weeks of less focused discussion.

As the leader, it is your responsibility to ensure that your group focuses on only one theme per week in order to guarantee that each individual wrestles as deeply as possible with the content of each chapter.

We pray that your group will be very fruitful. Thanks for loving Jesus and his people enough to spend time examining the most important message that has ever been shared.

In Christ,

Cole Brown

INTRODUCTION

We are blessed to live in a time of increased interest in what we call "the gospel." Contemporary Christianity is filled with people and movements calling for a "gospel-centered" approach to Christian life and ministry. We have entire networks of gospel-centered churches pastored by gospel-centered preachers who attended gospel-centered seminaries and have written gospel-centered books on everything from gospel-centered parenting to gospel-centered marriage to gospel-centered media consumption. We read these books and attend these churches while posting our gospel-centered social media updates, listening to our gospel-centered music, and seeking out gospel-centered conversations with our gospel-centered friends. When possible, we do all of this while wearing our gospel-centered clothing purchased from our gospel-centered online retailer of choice so we can rock our favorite gospel-centered style while doing our gospel-centered ministry. All of this is magnificent, and is evidence of a profound spiritual awakening happening right before our eyes.

But there's one problem: For all of contemporary Christianity's emphasis on being gospel-centered, there is still a lot of confusion about what the gospel we are so centered on actually *is*.

Just prior to writing this booklet, for example, I was in a room with roughly 40 other pastors. Each of these pastors is truly gospel-centered in that he faithfully proclaims the gospel from his pulpit and in his pastoral conversations every week. Yet when we were asked by our facilitator to answer the question "What is the gospel?" the answers provided by this group of faithful pastors were dishearteningly abstract and inconsistent:

hope
grace
faith alone
good news
love
mercy
forgiveness
redemption

All of these words are wonderful, biblical words with rich theological meaning; each and every one of them is closely related to the gospel. But not one of them *is* the gospel. Not one of them answers the question, "What is the gospel?" If even gospel-preaching pastors like these lack clarity on what exactly the gospel is, we should not be surprised to find that same confusion in the pews of even our most gospel-centered churches.

And this is not a minor concern. The Scriptures reveal it is the power of the gospel that saves us (makes us right with God) and the power of the gospel that sanctifies us (makes us more like Jesus). This means the gospel is of central importance for both eternity and the present moment. What could be more important, then, than having a clear understanding of exactly what the gospel is? What could be more important than being able to explain the gospel to others accurately and adequately?

If you're still reading then I wrote this booklet for you.

If you're a Christian, you need to know the gospel in such a way that you can preach it to yourself and preach it to others with confidence and with clarity. If you're already at that point, you need to meditate on the gospel again and again as an act of worship and repentance. It is my prayer that this brief booklet will help you to do all of the above.

If you're not a Christian, you need to know the gospel in such a way that you can respond to it with honesty and integrity. Before you accept or reject the gospel of Jesus Christ, you need to be sure you know it. If you're like I was at the age of twenty-one, it is very possible that the Christian gospel you have rejected up to this point in your life is not, in fact, the Christian gospel at all, but a message that's based on a false understanding of what the Bible teaches. It is my prayer that this brief booklet will help you know for certain the content of Jesus' message so your response, whatever it may be, is a response to the *actual* gospel, and not just an inaccurate or incomplete version of it.

In the pages that follow, I will begin by providing a one-sentence definition of the gospel as it is articulated in the Bible and as it has been understood by the Church throughout history. I will then explain each of the five components of the definition in its own chapter. My goal is not to provide the final word or the best word on what the gospel is; the Bible alone does both of those things. Instead, I want to provide a summary of the Bible's message that is simple enough to be easily memorized and reproduced, yet robust enough to take you deeper in your lifelong journey into the unfathomable riches of God's gospel.

But before we establish what the gospel *is*, let's establish what the gospel is *not* by looking at some common misunderstandings.

DISCUSSION GUIDE: INTRODUCTION

CHAPTER SUMMARY
We are blessed to live in a time of gospel awakening. Contemporary Christianity is filled with people and movements calling for a "gospel-centered" approach to Christian life and ministry. This is wonderful. Yet, unfortunately, for all of our emphasis on being gospel-centered, there is still a lot of confusion about what the gospel we are so centered on actually *is*.

INTRODUCTION
Have each group member introduce himself or herself and share a bit of his or her story. If your group consists of Christians, you may ask the participants to share the story of how they came to know Jesus and what they hope to get out of this study. If your group consists of non-Christians, you may ask them to explain why this topic interests them and what they hope to get out of it. The leader should share first, modeling honesty and vulnerability as she shares her own experience with the gospel, and then should encourage the other group members to share as much of their story as they are willing to share.

DISCUSSION QUESTIONS
1. What exposure, if any, have you had to the modern "gospel-centered" movement? What positives have you seen? What negatives or potential dangers have you seen?

2. The author says the purpose of this book is to clarify precisely what the gospel is as directly and simply as possible. If you had to give a definition for "the gospel" today, in five sentences or less, what would you say?

3. Read Romans 1:16 and Mark 16:15 out loud. Based on these verses and your own insight, why is a proper definition of the gospel essential for those who are already Christians? Why is it essential for those who are not yet Christians?

4. Read Colossians 1:21-23 out loud. According to this text, what are some of the promises of God that are contingent upon your faithfulness to the gospel?

5. Why have you chosen to read this book and participate in this study?

6. Are there any particular questions you have about the gospel or issues surrounding it that you hope the author answers? What are they, and why are they important to you?

CONCLUSION

Spend some time praying as a group for the study. Pray specifically for God to…

- …clarify His gospel in the weeks to come.

- …warm your hearts more and more to the gospel.

- …protect you from being disinterested or unmoved because you already know what the gospel is, and for him to cause you to be excited at the Good News instead, whether or not it is new to you.

...NOT WHAT WE OFTEN THINK

Nine years ago, I planted Emmaus Church in Portland, Oregon with a small but wonderful team of diverse people. Together, we were just beginning to understand the true nature of the gospel, and we could not wait to share what we were learning with our city. Before we began preaching the gospel as a church, though, we wanted to know what our Christian and non-Christian neighbors thought of when they heard the word "gospel."

So we took an informal survey by asking as many as we could, "What is the gospel?" The answers we received were revealing. Everyone was able to provide an answer, but almost none of the answers were heard were biblical. The following are just eight of the common answers we received then, and still receive today. These are things we often think when we hear the word "gospel" that are not, in fact, *the* gospel.

A Style of Music
Though there is a genre of music commonly referred to as "gospel music," the gospel is not a style of music. Ironically, the modern songs we label as "gospel" songs very rarely include the gospel in their lyrics at all. The most common themes in gospel music today include God's presence with us in the midst of life's troubles, God's goodness to us in general, and God's power at work in our lives. When approached biblically, each of these themes is good and true; however, not one of these is the gospel.

Four Books of the Bible
Though the books of Matthew, Mark, Luke, and John are commonly referred to as "The Gospels," these books themselves are not the gospel. They include the gospel, but they do not *only* include the gospel; they also include stories, facts, teachings, and details that are *not* the gospel. The answer to the question "What is the gospel?" is not answered by the statement "Caesar Augustus issued a decree that a census should be taken" or "It was full of large fish, 153." If we are looking for the gospel, we are not looking for these four books, we are looking for something specific that each of these four books communicates.

The Good News
The word "gospel" literally means "good news." Thus, the gospel is good news—but good news is not the gospel. Referring to the gospel as "good news" only tells us something about the quality of the message (it is good!); it does not tell us anything about the content of the message (why is it good?). To know *why* the gospel is good news, we have to know the content of the message and not just the quality of the message.

God Loves Us
Many of us may have been told that the good news of the gospel is that God loves us. It *is* true that God loves us, and this *is* good news. But we can be thankful it is not *the* good news, because it actually raises more questions than it answers: What does it *mean* that God loves me? *Why* does God love me? *How* does God love me? How can I know for sure that God loves me? Why does it matter that God loves me? "God loves us" is not the answer to the question

"What is the gospel?"; however, the gospel is the answer to every one of our questions about God's love.

Grace

The gospel and grace are often confused as one and the same thing, but they aren't. The gospel is the fullest *expression* of God's grace, but it is much more than just grace. Grace is typically defined as God's undeserved favor. As such, it is closely related to the gospel in that God's undeserved favor was a cause of the truths the gospel proclaims and a means by which we hear and respond to them. But God's undeserved favor is not itself the gospel.

Forgiveness of Sins

You may have heard it said that the gospel is simply the news that our sins are forgiven. It is true that the gospel and the forgiveness of sins are related, but the forgiveness of sins is not the only implication of the gospel. Instead, the forgiveness of sins is one of *many* results of the gospel. And this result is not something experienced by all; it is only experienced by those who respond to the gospel a certain way. Forgiveness of sins is in this one way contingent upon us, but the gospel is not contingent upon us in any way at all.

Hope

The gospel is a message that should produce hope in those who hear it and believe it, but that does not mean that a feeling of hope is itself the gospel. Hope, like the forgiveness of sins, is a *result* of the gospel, not its *content*. In fact, we can only truly hope after we have truly understood the gospel. Otherwise, we cannot know why we can hope, what we can hope for, or what we can hope in.

Living a Good Life
The most common answer we received as we asked people "What is the gospel?" was "living a good life." By this, people mean the good news is that God gives us the ability to live a moral life, or a prosperous life, or both. Because Christians have not done the best job of explaining what the gospel actually is, most non-Christians believe this is the core message of Christianity. This is why so many reject Christianity on the basis that they don't need religion or church—because they believe they can be good and happy without them.

But the gospel is not about morality or prosperity. By itself, that would not be good news. For those who already believe they are living such a life, the gospel would be irrelevant news, because they already have what the gospel offers. Meanwhile, for those who know they are not living such a life, the gospel would be condemning news, because though the gospel says they can do it, they are failing to do what it says they can do.

The gospel is something else. It most definitely has tremendous implications for your life. But it is not about your life, your morality, or your prosperity. It is about something infinitely greater than your life, your morality, and your prosperity.

So What is It?
What is the gospel if it is not what we often think it is? **The gospel is the good news of who Jesus is and what Jesus has done for the glory of God and for the good of God's people**. This is the one-sentence definition we will unpack in the remainder of this book.

DISCUSSION GUIDE: ...NOT WHAT WE OFTEN THINK

CHAPTER SUMMARY
When you ask people what the gospel is, you are likely to hear a number of responses that may sound right, but simply are not what the Bible defines as the gospel. Common answers include: the four books of the Bible, the good news, the message that God loves us, grace, forgiveness of sins, hope, and living the good life. Though all of these are related to the gospel in some way, none of them *is* the gospel. Instead, the author defines the gospel as "the good news of who Jesus is and what Jesus has done for the glory of God and for the good of God's people."

DISCUSSION QUESTIONS
1. Read Galatians 1:6-9 out loud. In your own words, what are some of the dangers and consequences of not holding to a biblical view of the gospel? Based on what we know about Paul and Paul's audience, who is vulnerable to accepting a twisted version of the gospel?

2. Read the next verse in Galatians, 1:10. What do you think is the relation between verses 6-9 and verse 10? Why?

3. The author of the book lists a number of things that are often mistaken for the gospel. Which of these have you seen confused with the gospel by others? Which have you personally

confused with the gospel? Did the author miss any misunderstandings that you have encountered? If so, what are they?

4. When non-Christians in your life think about the "core message of Christianity," what do they tend to think it is? Why?

5. In your life, what are some "gospels" you have put your trust in apart from the gospel of the Bible? What stories have you looked to for meaning? What pursuits have you given your time and energy to?

6. Looking at your own cultural environment, which "gospels" are most prevalent and why? What stories are the people around you trusting in to give their life meaning and joy?

7. Reread the one-sentence summary of the gospel provided in the book. What do you notice about the focus of this definition? What do you notice is absent?

CONCLUSION
Spend some time praying prayers of repentance and protection.

- REPENTANCE: Each group member should repent for the false gospels they have put their hope in and the things they have hoped in, trusted in, and pursued in place of Christ, as well as the ways they have lived to please other people instead of God.

- PROTECTION: Each group member should ask God to protect them from believing a twisted gospel as the Galatian Christians did, and to empower them to live for His pleasure instead of for the pleasure of others.

...THE GOOD NEWS...

We have already seen that good news is not the gospel, but the gospel is most definitely good news. In fact, it is more than good news—it is *the* good news. This is the very meaning of the word " gospel," and it teaches us two important things about what the gospel is.

Within the phrase "the good news," there is a definite article, a noun, and an adjective. I don't point this out because I think you're in need of a grade school grammar lesson; I point this out because each of these three simple parts of speech communicates something important about the gospel.

The noun, "news," tells us that this message is a report of a past event. It is this seemingly insignificant detail that actually separates the Christian gospel from every other religion on the planet. To paraphrase New York Pastor Tim Keller, Christianity offers good news, while every other religion offers good advice. The good advice of other religions (and irreligion) is a report of who you must be or what you must do in the future; the good news of Christianity is a report of who Jesus is and what Jesus has already done in the past. The two could not be more different. The message of good advice says the key to finding a fulfilling life, unity with God, and salvation from your biggest problem lies in your own ability to follow the advice. The message of good news, on the other hand, says the key to these things lies in what Jesus has already accomplished on your behalf.

This is one reason why the noun "news" is modified by the adjective "good": the adjective "good" tells us this report is worth celebrating. Adapting Keller's illustration will help us understand why: Imagine your nation is facing a great and terrible war like none you have ever known. This war directly affects you, your loved ones, your work, your home—everything. You are thirsty for victory, since you know your life and the future of everything you love depends on it. You're shaking with anxiety and have no idea what is happening or what you can do.

One day, then, you turn on the television and immediately hear Anderson Cooper announce, "We found the enemy's weakness and we know the way to victory. All you have to do is leave your home, risk your life, fight with everything you have, and do exactly as I say, and we can win." How would you feel? Mostly like, you'd experience a slight tinge of hope for potential victory, but also feel overwhelmed by a major sense of fear about what you have to do to achieve it—and whether or not you even *can*.

Now imagine that when you turned on the TV, you instead heard Anderson Cooper make a different announcement: "The war is over. The enemy has been fully and finally defeated. You may now live in peace and freedom." Now what would you feel? Odds are you'd be relieved and elated. You are not hearing a report about a potential victory in the future, but a report of a certain victory that has already been secured. You get to receive all the benefits of the victory without ever having to enter the battlefield yourself.

Most of the news you and I are accustomed to hearing is either bad news that feeds our anxiety and depression or lighter news that is essentially irrelevant to our day-to-day lives. This imaginary announcement from Anderson Cooper would be nothing like either; it would be truly and deeply good news that impacts us so personally that our entire lives would be forever changed in that instant.

The gospel of Jesus Christ is like that, only infinitely better.

The gospel is infinitely better because the victory Jesus won for us is a victory we could never win for ourselves. The reason we could never win is because our worst enemy in this war is not outside of us, but inside of us. The Bible calls this enemy "sin." Sin is our natural-born hunger to worship creation in place of the Creator, as well as the destructive attitudes and behaviors that this natural-born hunger produces. It leads us to give our love, trust, obedience, and fear to created people and things instead of to the Creator of those people and things. Its presence in us is so pervasive and so powerful that the Bible calls us "slaves to sin." All of this makes us both prisoners of war who cannot escape the clutches of the enemy and criminals of war who have joined forces with the enemy against God. We have no hope of victory over sin and no hope of peace with the God who made us and loves us.

It sounds hopeless. And apart from Jesus, it is hopeless.

Yet the more you understand how deeply hopeless your situation is apart from Jesus, the more you realize how profoundly *good* the good news of the gospel is. Because the gospel announces that at in the past, Jesus did something to solve both problems. So Jesus not only saves us from having to win the war ourselves (which is good news!), he saves us from losing the war we could never, ever win ourselves (which is even better news!).

The last part of speech in "the good news" is the definite article, "the." This simple three-letter-word tells us a lot. For starters, it tells us the gospel of Jesus Christ is a unique message: it is not *a* message of good news, it is *the* message of good news. Because it is *the* good news, we must be careful to not accept any substitute in its place.

There are and have always been imitation gospels, and believing one of these gospels can be so destructive that the Bible says those who preach them are to be accursed. For this reason, if you hear a gospel that is primarily about what you should do in the future instead of what Jesus has done in the past, you should reject it outright. It is not news, and is not *the* gospel—even if Jesus' name is a part of it. In the same way, if the Christian gospel you have heard sounds like a reason to grieve or fear instead of reason to celebrate, you may not have heard *the* gospel—even if Jesus' name is a part of it. *The* gospel is and will always be good news.

While there are many pieces of good news, there is no piece of good news even remotely as meaningful or powerful as this one. In the next chapter, then, we will begin to identify the specific content of this unique message.

DISCUSSION GUIDE: …THE GOOD NEWS…

CHAPTER SUMMARY
Though good news is not the content of the gospel, the content of the gospel is most certainly good news. More than that, it is *the* good news. The fact that it is "news" tells us that it is about a past event that has already occurred; the fact that it is "good" tells us this past act has positive and present implications for us; and the definite article "the" tells us there are no alternatives to or substitutions for this message.

DISCUSSION QUESTIONS
1. What are some of the implications of the fact that the gospel is a message about an event completed in the past, as opposed to something that might be or must be completed in the future?

2. What are some examples of gospels that are more about what remains to be done in the future than what has already been done in the past?

3. In an earlier discussion, we talked about the various "gospels" of our culture. What were some of the ones we discussed? Examine them. Are they primarily about something that was achieved in the past, or something that must be achieved in the future? Analyze and explain the similarities and differences you see between them.

4. According to the author, what are some of the reasons that the gospel is *good* news? What else might you add to what was mentioned?

5. Read Ephesians 2:1-5 and Titus 3:3-7 out loud. What do the structures of these two passages have in common? Why is this important?

6. How are we both prisoners of war and criminals of war, according to the author and/or to Scripture?

7. What are some of the dangers of emphasizing the bad news brought on by sin more than the good news delivered through Jesus Christ? How have you experienced this overemphasis of the bad news in your lifetime?

8. What are some of the dangers of emphasizing the good news delivered through Jesus Christ without understanding the bad news brought on by sin? How have you experienced this underemphasis of the bad news in your lifetime?

CONCLUSION

Spend some time praying prayers of praise and thanksgiving in response to being reminded that the gospel is good news to your ears.

- PRAISE: Each one should praise God for who He is and for being a God who sends us the good news of what has already been done instead of bad news of what we must do.

- THANKSGIVING: Each one should thank God for choosing to win a victory for us that we could have never won for ourselves.

...OF WHO JESUS IS...

If the good news of the gospel were to appear on the front page of your local newspaper, the headline would begin, "GOOD NEWS: Jesus Christ is fully God and fully human." Or, if you're one of the millions who prefer to receive their good news online, you might see #JesusIsFullyGodAndFullyHuman as the #1 trending topic on your twitter timeline. Upon reading this headline for the first time, you would likely have two questions: First, why is the identity of a man who lived in a small town over 2,000 years ago newsworthy? And second, why is his identity considered to be such *good* news? The answer to both questions is in the details.

Jesus is God.

Along with God the Father and God the Holy Spirit, Jesus possesses the nature and attributes of the One True God. He is eternal; there has never been and will never be a moment in which Jesus did not or does not exist. He is omniscient (all-knowing); there is not a fact nor a potential fact of the past, present, or future that Jesus does not fully and presently know. He is omnipotent (all-powerful); he can do all things and cannot be overcome by anything. He is omnipresent (all-present); there is not the smallest corner of our universe or any other in which Jesus is not personally and currently present. He is holy; he is utterly unlike anyone or anything else and is morally pure in every possible way without even the slightest stain of imperfection. He is Creator; everything that has ever been brought into existence was done so by Jesus. He is Sustainer; everything that continues to exist does so by his will and his word. By virtue of all of the above, he is also Judge; everything he has made, both seen and unseen, must give an account to him for what it has done with the existence he has generously granted it.

This is good news.

The fact that Jesus is God is good news because it allows us to *know* God. Every other religious leader offers to *tell us* about God. Jesus offers to *show us* God, up close and personal. He does this by showing us himself. "I and the Father are one," he says, "If you have seen me, you have seen the Father." We no longer have to guess what God is like, nor is our knowledge of him restricted only to what we can observe from a distance. Because Jesus is God, we can look at Jesus and see God for ourselves, precisely as he is. This is good news!

Also, the fact that Jesus is God is also good news because only an infinite God could bear the weight of our infinite sin. Contrary to popular belief, the thing God calls "sin" is not primarily a behavioral issue. It is primarily a relational issue. You were made by God and you are daily sustained by God. Everything you have and everything you are is due to his faithfulness to you. You sin when you respond to his faithfulness with unfaithfulness by giving your trust, your love, or your obedience to someone or something in God's place. For example, when you look to the things you accomplish in life to make you feel valuable or important, you are trusting in the things you do instead of trusting in the God who gives you the ability to do them. When the primary object of your heart's affection is a human being (be it yourself or another) or a thing (like money or comfort), you are loving something God made more than you love the God who made it. And when you obey what your body says *feels* right or what your culture says *is* right, you allow yourself to be mastered by something other than your Master. Thus, sin includes both doing the wrong thing *and* doing the right thing for the wrong reasons. You have done this—whether through the thoughts of your mind, affections of your heart, words of your mouth or deeds of your body—and continue to do this.

In most cases, your sin victimizes other people; in every case, your sin victimizes the God to whom you owe your existence and from whom you receive every good thing you have. And because God is the primary and constant victim of your sin, he is the only one who can forgive your sin and release you from its consequences. Yet because God is also both holy and Judge, he cannot ignore your evil. The only way he can forgive you of your sin and release you from its consequences is if your sin and its consequences are placed on someone else. Yet who can bear the weight of your infinite sin against the infinite God? Only the infinite God himself—which is exactly who Jesus is. Because Jesus is God, your sin can be dealt with through God-on-God wrath instead of God-on-you wrath. This is good news!

The fact that Jesus is God is also good news because it allows us to know that everything he says is *certain* (because he is all-knowing and holy) and everything he does is *perfect* (because he is all-powerful and holy). This means when Jesus says he has come to fulfill God's Law in our place and on our behalf, we can be sure he did it, and did so perfectly. Jesus did not leave any portion of God's Law unfulfilled; he did not overlook even the smallest command for even the slightest moment, or give his trust, love or obedience to anyone other than God the Father. It also means that when Jesus went to the cross to receive God the Father's judgment in our place and on our behalf and said, "It is finished," it was truly finished. He did not leave a single one of his people unatoned for or a single one of our sins unpaid for. This is good news!

Jesus is Human.

Like you and I, Jesus was born of a woman. He lived as a baby, completely dependent on others for his physical sustenance and safety. He grew as a child, developing physically, mentally, and emotionally. He lived as a man, working just as we work, sleeping just as we sleep, praying just as we pray, loving just as we love, weeping just as we weep, fearing as we fear, and being tempted in every way just as we are tempted. He experienced the same joys we experience, he felt the same suffering we feel, he possessed the same relationships we possess, with all of their highs and each of their lows. He even tasted the same fate as every other human who has ever lived: death.

This is good news.

The fact that Jesus is human is good news because only a human being can empathize with the human experience. Other religions offer us a God who cannot know what it is like to be human. Yet these gods nevertheless place demands on our humanity. Jesus, on the other hand, is a God who experientially knows our humanity because he himself *is* human. Because of this, Jesus can sympathize and empathize with us as we try to live in God's world in God's way. Whether you are tempted to sin, frozen by fear, assaulted by suffering, or exhausted by life, Jesus the human understands and Jesus the God responds according to that understanding. This is good news!

What's more, the fact that Jesus is human is good news because only a human being can serve as a substitute for another human being. For your record of sin to be replaced with a record of righteousness, a human being would have to live a life of human perfection as your substitute. For the punishment for your infinite sin to be transferred to another, an innocent human being would have to willfully take your punishment upon himself. For your slavery to death to become the liberty of eternal life, a human being would have to defeat death by falling under its power and then rising again as your substitute. Yet what human being can live a life of perfection, willfully take the punishment for your sin, and walk out of his own grave? Only a human being who is also God—which is exactly who Jesus is. This is good news!

Before I became a Christian in my early twenties, everything I knew about Jesus came from Christmas nativity scenes and episodes of *South Park*. Though your thoughts about Jesus may have less embarrassing origins, most of us have had our understanding of who Jesus is at least partially shaped by sources outside of the Bible. As a result, it is not uncommon for people to know all sorts of things about Jesus without ever knowing who Jesus is: *Jesus is fully God and fully man.* This is not just a seven-word answer to a theological question; it is one-half of the content of *the* good news that has changed individuals, communities, and the world since the day it was first proclaimed nearly 2,000 years ago.

It can change you too.

DISCUSSION GUIDE: ...OF WHO JESUS IS...

CHAPTER SUMMARY
Part of the content of the good news is that Jesus is both 100% God and 100% human. It is good news that Jesus is God because this means God is knowable and because only an infinite God could bear the weight of our infinite sin. Also, the fact that Jesus is God is good news because it means everything he tells us is certain and everything he does is perfect. Meanwhile, it is good news that Jesus is human because only a human being can empathize with our human experience and serve as our substitute through his perfect life, sacrificial death, and victorious resurrection.

DISCUSSION QUESTIONS
1. How would you summarize the good news that Jesus is fully God?

2. How would you summarize the good news that Jesus is fully human?

3. Have you personally tended to emphasize the god-ness of Jesus or the humanity of Jesus? What do you think you may have missed out on by emphasizing one aspect of His being over the other?

4. Which is more difficult for you to wrap your head around: that Jesus is 100% God or that Jesus is 100% human? Why?

5. Read Hebrews 1:1-3 out loud. What does this tell us about the god-ness of Jesus in relation to the god-ness of God the Father?

6. As you look at Jesus and listen to Jesus in the Scriptures, what do you learn about who God is and what God is like? Share as many specifics as you can.

7. Read Hebrews 4:15-16 out loud. How could/should this encourage you in your moments of weakness? Be as specific as possible.

8. The author acknowledges that prior to becoming a Christian, everything he knew about Jesus came from sources outside of the Bible. Where has your information about Jesus come from? Share as many sources as you can think of. After reading this chapter, do you need to make changes to your understanding of who Jesus is?

CONCLUSION

Have each person pray for the person to their right. Specifically, have them ask God to help them...

A. ...know God as He is more and more by looking at and listening to Jesus in the Bible.

B. ...find comfort in their moments of questioning, temptation and suffering in the fact that Jesus understands them because He lived what they are living and He can help them because He overcame it.

...AND WHAT JESUS HAS DONE...

Our news channels and social media feeds are filled with announcements of what this person or that person has done. Many of these events are negative, the few positive things rarely have lasting importance, and even less have any personal relevance for us. None of them—not even one—transforms the trajectory of the entire universe. Only what Jesus has done accomplishes that. This is why the content of the good news of the gospel has a second half. After proclaiming who Jesus is, the gospel proclaims what Jesus has done.

Jesus Lived Perfectly
As the God-man, Jesus lived a life of absolute perfection. This is easy to say, but hard to comprehend, as we have never even seen a truly good life, much less a truly perfect life. While our minds think evil thoughts, his mind thought only pure thoughts, without exception. While our mouths speak lies and damages people, his mouth spoke only truth and restored people. While our hearts love what they should hate and hate what they should love, his heart was permanently fixed in worship on God the Father and perpetually reflected His affections. While our bodies have rushed to do evil and repeatedly yielded to their temptations, his body resisted all evil and did only righteousness—ever.

Jesus lived in this way as a child, as a teenager, and as an adult. This was his way of life when he was supported by others, and even when he was ridiculed, abandoned, and betrayed by others. His spotless living was the same when he could sense the Father's immediate presence as it was when the Father's presence was nowhere to be found. It is because of this perfect life of obedience that the gospel proclaims the good news: Jesus has fulfilled God's Law at every point and in every way, and he has done it in your place and for your benefit.

Jesus Died Sacrificially
As the God-man, Jesus died the most horrific death that anyone ever has died or ever will die. He died by crucifixion, being stripped of his clothes and publicly nailed to a wooden cross, which is one of the most painful and shameful ways for anyone to die. Yet untold thousands of others have experienced that same painful and shameful death by crucifixion. As horrible as the method of Jesus' death was, there were other factors that make his death the worst of all deaths.

First, Jesus is the only truly righteous person to ever die. Roughly 153,000 people die every day, yet not one of these people has ever died righteous. Every one has died as a sinner who has fallen immeasurably short of the demands of God's Law. Even those who die so young that they have never consciously sinned do not die free of a sinful nature or full of righteous living. Only Jesus died as both innocent (having never done wrong) and righteous (having only done right). This is one reason that Jesus' death is the most horrific of all deaths, because it is the most unjust of all deaths.

Second, Jesus is the only person to die bearing God's wrath for the sins of the whole world. Every person who has ever died has died awaiting a future date when they will stand before God and receive his just judgment. Yet Jesus faced the holy judgment of God in full as he still lived, hanging on the cross. Even worse, he faced the holy judgment of God not for his own sins (he had none), but for all of the sins of all of God's people throughout all of time. This is why Jesus repeatedly threw himself to the ground and sweated drops of blood the evening before his death—not because he feared the physical pain of crucifixion, which many had tasted before him, but because he feared the spiritual pain of being cut off from the God of all light and life and bearing the full brunt of his wrath for every one of the sins of every one of his people who would ever live. Though Jesus had never sinned and had only lived in perfect righteousness, Jesus became sin for us and was consumed by the fire of God's wrath. This is the second reason that Jesus' death is the most horrific of all deaths— because it was the only death died under the full weight of God's punishment for all sin!

You may be wondering why something so unjust and so terrible would be included as part of "the good news." The reason is because Jesus did not die this most horrific death because *he* deserved it, but because *you* deserved it. His death was a sacrificial death intended to absorb God's wrath so God's people would not have to. It is because of this horrific sacrificial death that the gospel proclaims the good news: the innocent and righteous Jesus has died terribly under God's judgment, and he has done it in your place and for your benefit.

Jesus Rose Victoriously

As the God-man, three days after he was swallowed by the grave, Jesus swallowed death itself in victory. Though his death was confirmed by both friendly and unfriendly witnesses, his body prepared for burial by friends, and a stone rolled in front of his tomb and guarded by Roman soldiers, Jesus stood up and walked out of his grave three days later, never to return. What appeared to be Jesus' defeat by sin, satan and death on Friday was revealed as his triumph over sin, satan and death on Sunday. Over the next forty days, he showed himself to dozens of witnesses as the Risen Son of God. His followers who previously grieved now rejoiced. Many skeptics who previously doubted or outright denied now believed. Because of this miraculous event, the gospel proclaims the good news: the same Jesus who was laid in the grave is now and forever alive.

Jesus Ascended Finally
As the God-man, forty days after Jesus rose from the dead, he ascended into heaven, returning to the glory he had with the Father before time began. After his followers watched him ascend, Jesus sat down at the right hand of God the Father. In sitting down, he showed that he had finished all the work he came to earth to accomplish. In sitting at God's right hand, he showed that the crucified peasant is now enthroned with power and authority over all and he will one day return for his people. This is why the gospel proclaims the good news: Jesus has ascended into heaven where he now sits in The Father's presence, in our place and for our benefit, as he rules over us as our King until the day he returns for us.

The truths of who Jesus is and what Jesus has done together make up the entirety of the gospel. There is nothing that needs to be added to them. As we saw earlier, this is what makes the gospel *the* good news. It is a message of what *someone else* has already been and already done for us instead of a message of what *we* must be or do. This allows us to simply rest and receive the news with joy and gratitude. If we do, we will have eyes of faith to see that while the gospel is completed, the work of the gospel is not. It is still doing magnificent things.

DISCUSSION GUIDE: ...AND WHAT JESUS HAS DONE...

CHAPTER SUMMARY
While the first half of the good news proclaims who Jesus is, the second half proclaims what Jesus has done: live perfectly as our representative, die sacrificially as our substitute, rise victoriously as our hero, and ascend finally where He now sits at God's right hand, having completed His redemptive work on our behalf. The truths of who Jesus is and what Jesus has done together make up the content of the gospel. There is nothing that needs to be added to them. This is what makes the gospel such good news.

DISCUSSION QUESTIONS
1. How would you summarize the good news of what Jesus has done in your own words?

2. In the last chapter, we saw that Jesus is tempted in all the same ways we are. Yet in this chapter, we see that He lived without sin. Why is it important that we give equal attention to both? What do we lose if we emphasize his perfect obedience without his human temptation? What do we lose if we emphasize his human temptation without emphasizing his perfect obedience?

3. Read 1 John 3:5 out loud. What is the relationship between the passage's first affirmation and the second?

4. The author says that Jesus' death was the worst of all deaths. Yet it wasn't the horrific physical pain that made his death the worst of all deaths. According to the author, why *was* Jesus' death the worst of all deaths? What is your emotional response to these claims?

5. Read 2 Corinthians 5:21 and 1 Peter 3:18 as a group. What are the central arguments that both passages share in common? What do they tell us about Jesus? About us? About the results of His death? Why would this be considered good news?

6. Read Ephesians 1:19-23. What happened as a result of Jesus' ascension? Why is this good news for the world? For you?

7. The author claims that the content of the gospel can be completely and accurately summarized by explaining who Jesus is and what Jesus has done. What were you expecting to see him include as part of the gospel content that he didn't? Why?

CONCLUSION
Spend time praying prayers of praise and thanksgiving.

- PRAISE: Praise Jesus for being your sinless King, for reigning righteously over the whole universe in His power and goodness.

- THANKSGIVING: Thank Jesus for living the perfect life that you could not live and for dying the death under God's judgment that you deserved to die. Thank Him for defeating death, which you could never do yourself.

...FOR THE GLORY OF GOD...

The good news of who Jesus is and what Jesus has done is so terrifically *good* that you can't help but ask...

Why?

Why would God the Son willfully, voluntarily, and intentionally leave his heavenly throne, come to a broken earth, live a life of suffering, be unjustly condemned, and die under the awesome power of God's terrifying wrath? Why would he do this at all? More than that, why would he do this in place of us, his enemies?

This is a very reasonable question. It is also one God anticipates we will ask, and he answers it for us in two parts. The first part of the answer is, "for the glory of God." Jesus did what he did to call attention to the magnificence of who God is.

To Glorify God's Mercy
The message of who Jesus is and what Jesus has done brings glory to God's mercy. As human beings, we naturally respond to our enemies in one of two ways: fight or flight. That is, we either turn our hearts, words, and actions against them in order to hurt them, or we turn ourselves away from them in order to protect ourselves. The gospel of Jesus shows us that God is unlike us, because he does neither of these things. Instead of turning his anger against us, God turned his anger upon himself in our place. Instead of

turning away from us, God came near to us clothed in human flesh.

This is mercy unequaled, and Jesus did what he did in order to shine a bright light on this aspect of who God is.

To Glorify God's Grace

The gospel shows off not only God's mercy (his choice to withhold from us the punishment we *do* deserve), but also his grace (his choice to give to us the reward we do *not* deserve). We do not deserve for God the Son to come to us in the person of Jesus Christ. We do not deserve for him to live perfectly in our place, die sacrificially in our place, rise victoriously on our behalf, or ascend into heaven to rule as our King. We also do not deserve the countless benefits we receive as a result of who Jesus is and what Jesus has done. Yet God nonetheless gives us all of these things, freely, even though it costs him everything.

This is grace incomprehensible, and Jesus did what he did in order to draw attention to this magnificent quality of God's character.

To Glorify God's Righteousness

While the message of the gospel shows us God's mercy and God's grace, it does not leave us believing that God overlooks evil or is soft on sin. In fact, it does the exact opposite: It shows off God's righteousness. It shows us God would rather be personally punished for evil himself than to leave even the smallest evil unpunished. The work of Jesus assures us that every sin of the past, every sin of the present, and every sin of the future will be judged justly and fully by God—even if that judgment has to fall on his own innocent

Son. The most righteous human being in the history of the world would not come even remotely close to being this committed to righteousness.

This is righteousness unblemished, and Jesus did what he did in order to display this wondrous attribute of God.

To Glorify Himself

Why would God the Son do what he did? The Scriptures reveal repeatedly that the first and primary reason Jesus did what he did was to glorify God the Father and, in return, for God the Father to glorify him. This happens as the gospel functions as a spotlight that allows us to see who God is with clarity. When we see him under the spotlight of the gospel, our appropriate response is praise and worship. This is exactly what God intends to obtain through the gospel.

This might make you uncomfortable; after all, we tend to think it is morally wrong for someone to seek their own glory. Yet this is because we misunderstand why most glory-seeking is wrong. What makes glory-seeking morally wrong is when the glory being sought is not God's glory. As God, he deserves all glory. This is why human beings' pursuit of their own glory is hideous, yet God's desire for his own glory is beautiful. The difference is that as the Creator of all things, he deserves *all* glory, and as creatures who owe our existence to him, we deserve none.

It is not wrong for God to be primarily motivated by his own glory; in fact, it would be wrong for God to be primarily motivated by anything other than his own glory. If he were to do anything *primarily* for someone or something other than himself, then he would be prizing that someone or something as higher than himself. While that is virtuous for humans, it is not virtuous for God, as valuing anyone or anything above him is the very root of all sin.

Not only is it not wrong for God to be primarily motivated by his own glory, but it is also loving. We benefit tremendously from God's glory; as he is glorified through the gospel, we get to see God as he is. We get to marvel at his mercy, grace, and righteousness. We get to have our lives reoriented around his glory (which brings us true life) instead of having our lives oriented around our own glory (which destroys our life). If the gospel you have heard is a gospel that is first and primarily about how it benefits you, it is not *the* gospel. *The* gospel glorifies God before it does anything else.

DISCUSSION GUIDE: …FOR THE GLORY OF GOD…

CHAPTER SUMMARY

The good news of who Jesus is and what Jesus has done is so incredibly good that you can't help but ask why God the Son would willfully, voluntarily and intentionally do all that he did in the place of us, his enemies. The Bible answers that question by telling us he primarily did it for God's glory. Specifically, he did it to glorify God's mercy, God's grace, God's righteousness, and ultimately to glorify himself.

DISCUSSION QUESTIONS

1. Which of the character qualities of God in this chapter most causes you to marvel: his mercy, grace, righteousness, or commitment to his own glory? Why?

2. In what ways are grace and mercy different? In what ways are they similar?

3. Based on what is discussed in this chapter, how would you answer someone who says God is evil for demanding his own glory?

4. Read Romans 3:21-28 together. According to these verses, in what specific ways does Jesus glorify God's mercy, grace and righteousness? Spend time examining Paul's line of argument and its implications.

5. Read Romans 9:22-23 and Ephesians 1:4-6 aloud. Both of these passages speak of the common theme of God's glory, but in a very different way. What are the similarities in the passages? What are the differences?

6. Read Revelation 5:6-14, a song of praise sung to "The Lamb" (Jesus Christ). What are the reasons given here that Jesus is worthy of glory? What are the things that motivate the praises of this song?

CONCLUSION

Spend time praying prayers of praise for the many ways in which the gospel glorifies God. If possible, sing a song that focuses on God's character and glory, like that of Revelation 5:6-14.

...AND FOR THE GOOD OF GOD'S PEOPLE.

The message of who Jesus is and what Jesus has done is so staggering that it requires an explanation. Why would Jesus do *that* in place of us, his enemies? The Bible tells us that the primary reason he did what he did was for the glory of God. But while the glory of God is the *primary* reason Jesus did what he did, the glory of God is not the *only* reason Jesus did what he did. He also did it for the good of God's people.

He did it for you.

The Scriptures testify that God the Father sent God the Son because he loves you, and God the Son came because he loves you. In every step of obedience that Jesus took in your place, Jesus was motivated by God's love for God's people. With every sip of God's wrath that Jesus swallowed in your place, Jesus was motivated by God's love for God's people. Just as Jesus knew his work would bring much glory to God, he also knew it would bring much good to God's people.

The Good of Becoming God's Sons
One way the gospel brings good to God's people is by transforming God's enemies into God's sons. Those who place their trust in the good news of who Jesus is and what Jesus has done are adopted into God's family and given the title "son." This does not mean females suddenly cease being female and become male; rather, it means men and women suddenly cease being divided from God as the objects of his

wrath and instead become united to God as the objects of his blessing. This stunning change of identity from enemies to sons is possible because Jesus' work purchased both forgiveness and righteousness for his people. Through his perfect life, Jesus earned a record of spotless righteousness, which he transfers to those who trust in him. Furthermore, through his sacrificial death, Jesus paid the penalty for our past, present, and future sin, which he allowed to be transferred to him. To put it simply, Jesus was treated as God's enemy so we could be treated as God's sons.

This gift of sonship gives God's people both intimacy and security. Through faith in the gospel, we can experience the intimacy of knowing God as both *the* Father and *our* Father. As our Father, he speaks to us, listens to us, and guides us. He also simply enjoys us and invites us to simply enjoy him.

Through trusting in the gospel, we can also experience the security of knowing God adopted us as his own. We do not have to fear that he will stop loving us, stop accepting us, or stop blessing us if we say or do the wrong things. If our faith is in Jesus, we know God chose us and will always love us, accept us, and bless us simply because we are his.

The Good of Being Reshaped in God's Image
A second way the gospel brings good to God's people is by reshaping fallen people into the image of Jesus Christ. Those who place their trust in the good news of who Jesus is and what Jesus has done are not only forgiven of sin, but also freed from sin. From the moment of our birth, we are held tightly in sin's unyielding grip—so much so that the Bible calls us all

"slaves to sin." Even if we wanted to be free from its rule over us, we could not escape. Because of this, we fail miserably at what we were created to do: reflect God's image. We are selfish, while God is selfless. We are greedy, while God is generous. We are impure, while God is pure. We are vengeful, while God is just. We are impatient, while God is patient. We divide, while God unites. We avoid, while God pursues. We are liars, while God is the truth. We use our words to tear down, while God uses his words to build up. We aim to be served, while God aims to serve. We sinfully lust for our own glory, while God righteously seeks God's glory. Through our behavior, our words, and our affections, we spend our lives giving a very inaccurate picture of who God is.

Yet the gospel changes this. Forever.

First, the gospel frees us *from* slavery to sin by robbing sin of its power. When we place our faith in Jesus Christ, our sin and its judgment are removed from us and redistributed to Jesus. Sin had the power to rule us, yet it no longer has this power because Jesus died under its rule in our place. Sin had the power to condemn us, yet it no longer has this power because Jesus was condemned for us. The Bible explains that those who trust in Jesus are so deeply united to him that the person we used to be died when he died, and sin has no power over the dead.

Second, the gospel frees us *to* slavery to righteousness by giving us new life. In addition to dying with Jesus, those who place their faith in him are so deeply united to him that they also rise with Jesus. This new life comes with a new nature, a new heart, and a new power. Our new nature is a slave to righteousness, while our old nature was a slave to sin. Our new heart desires God's glory and pleasure above all else, while our old nature desired our own glory and pleasure above all else. Our new power comes in the form of God the Holy Spirit, who lives in us and empowers us to live as Jesus lived, while our old power came in the form of our own human ability, with all its weaknesses and limitations.

The Holy Spirit now works through our new nature and new heart to progressively make us more and more like Jesus Christ in our behavior, our words, and our affections. This reshaping is a process that takes time, but it is a process God promises to complete in every one of his people.

The Good of Being a Resident of God's City
A third way the gospel brings good to God's people is by making residents of this broken world into residents of God's eternal city. When God created the world, he created a paradise. In this paradise, human beings lived in perfect relationship with God, each other, and all of Creation. Yet when Adam and Eve chose to serve sin instead of God, this paradise was lost. Human beings fell out of right relationship with God, with each other, and with all of Creation. Every one of us born since has been born into an environment of sin and death, pain and shame, distance and division. We have been cast out of paradise and are powerless to return to it.

But Jesus is not powerless.

He entered into our broken world so he could bring us into his perfect world. He does this in two ways. One way he does this is by bringing us into paradise. The good news of the gospel tells us Jesus currently sits in the presence of God the Father. If we are united to Jesus through faith, then we too currently sit in the presence of God the Father, even as we live on earth. This means we are able to experience the paradise of being in right relationship with God. If we are united to Jesus through faith, we are also united to every other person in history who is united to Jesus through faith. This means we are able to experience the paradise of being in right relationship with each other through our membership in God's Church. Lastly, if our faith is in Jesus, we give our love, trust, fear, and obedience to the Creator of all things instead of to created things. This means we are able to experience the paradise of being in right relationship with Creation instead of being mastered by it.

A second way Jesus brings us out of this broken world and into his perfect world is by bringing paradise to us. The good news of the gospel tells us Jesus is already bringing small tastes of paradise to us now and will one day return to Earth to fully and finally restore paradise forever. In this fully restored paradise, there will be no sin and no death, no pain and no shame, no distance and no division. Those who have responded to the gospel in faith will see God face-to-face and will live in perfect relationship with God, each other, and all of creation as eternal residents of God's eternal city.

The glory of God alone would be reason enough for Jesus to do what he did, but it was not the only reason; he also did it for the good of God's people. All of these wonderful things are made available because of the gospel and are given as a free gift to any and all who respond to it in faith. The fact that God would freely give these blessings to people who don't deserve any of them brings God even more glory.

DISCUSSION GUIDE: ...AND FOR THE GOOD OF GOD'S PEOPLE.

CHAPTER SUMMARY
While the primary reason Jesus did what He did was the glory of God, the glory of God is not the only reason; he also did it for the good of God's people. He did it for you. Through who He is and what He did, we receive the good of becoming God's sons, of being reshaped into God's image, and of being residents of God's City. All of these things are made available because of the gospel and are given as a free gift to any and all who respond to it in faith.

DISCUSSION QUESTIONS
1. In your own words, why did Jesus do what He did for us?

2. Read 1 John 3:1-3 and Romans 8:15-16. According to these verses, what are some of the benefits of being made into God's sons? Which of these benefits most causes you to marvel? Why?

3. Apart from Christ's work, we would all remain slaves to sin. In what ways have you experienced this slavery—that is, the inability to change your affections, thoughts or behavior patterns?

4. Read Revelation 21:1-7 and 21-27. In these passages, we see a vivid description of the paradise Jesus gives to his people. Based on

this description, what can we expect to see and experience? What can we expect to no longer see and experience?

5. Which aspects of the coming paradise do you most look forward to? Why?

CONCLUSION

Spend time praying prayers of thanksgiving and request.

- THANKSGIVING: Thank God for the many gifts that He freely gives to us as a result of the gospel. Focus especially on those which feel most personal to you in this moment.

- REQUEST: Ask God to give you a greater awareness of and appreciation for the many things you receive as a result of the gospel. Ask Him to help you grow in gratitude for all He gives you.

NOW WHAT?

The gospel is the good news of who Jesus is and what Jesus has done for the glory of God and the good of God's people. This book may be the first time you have been exposed to this message or had it explained in detail, or it may be a message you've known for some time but need to be reminded of and energized by. Either way, the natural question that arises after reflecting on the gospel is, "What now?" The answer to that question is the same for those who have never responded to the gospel as it is for those who have, the same answer Jesus gave when he started preaching the good news: repent and believe.

The good news of the gospel is not the sort of news you can listen to and then go about living your life as normal; it demands a response. The first response the gospel demands is repentance. To "repent" simply means to change your mind and turn around. The proper response to the gospel, then, is to change your mind about who you are living your life for and turn around toward Jesus. You repent when you decide you are no longer the god of your own life and instead turn to Jesus as the God of your life.

The second response the gospel demands is belief. The type of belief the gospel requires has two elements: agreement and trust. Those who believe in the gospel agree with what it says about who Jesus is, what Jesus has done, and why Jesus did it. They also trust in these things by placing their life, death, emotions, and decisions in the hands of Jesus' work and Jesus' teaching. The first element of belief is like saying, "I believe marriage is a good thing." This is a right and true statement, yet just agreeing this is true is not the kind of faith the gospel demands. It also demands the second element of belief, which is like saying, "I do." The person with this sort of faith does not merely agree that marriage is good, but also believes it enough to shape their whole life around that belief.

You may be waiting for me to add a third response; maybe you're asking, "what else?" Perhaps you have heard that Christians have to live a certain way, worship a certain way, dress a certain way, or vote a certain way in order to be welcomed into God's family. But the truth is, there is no third response. Jesus calls you to respond to the gospel by repenting and believing. This is not just the door into the Christian life—it is the Christian life. Those who respond to the gospel once by repenting and believing are committing to a lifetime of repenting and believing as they constantly re-orient their lives around Jesus and his gospel. This is why the answer to the "What now?" question is the same for both non-Christians and Christians.

Though repentance and belief are a lifelong process, there are some immediate and permanent changes that occur the first time you respond to the gospel. First, those who respond to the gospel in repentance and faith are immediately and permanently transferred from the rule of darkness to light, from the kingdom of satan to Jesus, from spiritual death to spiritual life. Second, those who respond to the gospel in repentance and faith immediately and permanently become part of a new humanity with a new mission. This new humanity is created by Jesus and for Jesus and consists of people of every nation, culture, language, and status. Its members are so intimately united to each other and to Jesus that together they are called "the Body of Christ." Together they have the new mission of making Jesus known to the world so more and more people may be see the glory of God and receive the good he gives to his people.

The new humanity accomplishes this new mission by declaring the gospel with their words to friends, family, co-workers, and strangers. They also accomplish this new mission by demonstrating the power of the gospel through their participation in local churches. As Christians gather in local churches, they provide a living, breathing demonstration of how the gospel restores people to right relationship with God and each other. This happens as they forgive one another, serve one another, speak the truth to one another, give generously to one another, and simply live together—all because of the gospel.

If you have responded to the gospel in repentance and faith, you are now a privileged member of this new humanity. I pray you will express and experience that by being a member of a local church where this gospel is preached. Even if you do not yet respond to the gospel in repentance and faith, I pray you still find a local church where you can continue to hear the gospel and see its work in action. It is through the Body of Christ gathered in local churches—even with all of their flaws—that Jesus makes himself known to us.

While this is the end of the book, it is not the end of the matter. **The gospel is the good news of who Jesus is and what Jesus has done for the glory of God and for the good of God's people**. May we all begin and continue to repent and believe in response to it.

DISCUSSION GUIDE: NOW WHAT?

The gospel is the good news of who Jesus is and what Jesus has done for the glory of God and the good of God's people. This is not the sort of message you can simply hear; it requires a response. The specific response it requires is two-fold: repent and believe. This is the whole of the response that God requires to his glorious gospel. It is not merely the doorway into the Christian life—it *is* the Christian life. This is why the answer to the "What now?" question is the same for both Christians and non-Christians alike. Those who choose to respond in this way are immediately transferred from spiritual death to spiritual life and are made part of a new community which carries a new mission: the spread of the gospel.

DISCUSSION QUESTIONS
1. Now that you have finished the book, did you find that the gospel explained in the book was the same or different from the understanding of the gospel you had when you began? Explain.

2. Have you personally responded to this gospel in faith? Explain your answer.

3. Have you personally responded to this gospel in repentance? Explain your answer.

4. Whether you are a Christian or not, do you believe you are being called by God to

respond to the gospel in any specific way? Explain.

5. What questions about the gospel remain unanswered? What things discussed in this book would you like to learn more about?

6. Do you think this book might be helpful for someone you know? Who? Would you be willing to invite them to read it and discuss it with you?

7. Are you already an active member of a local church? If so, why? If not, why not?

8. Read 1 Peter 2:4-5, 9-10. What does this passage tell you about what God thinks of the local church? There is a lot here, so make as many observations as you can.

CONCLUSION
Have each person pray for the person on their right based on the answers to the above questions. For example, if someone has chosen to respond to the gospel in faith and repentance, spend time thanking God for what He is doing in them. If he or she has chosen to try to study the book with someone else, pray God will move the person/people he or she invites to participate with them. If someone has not found a local church where he or she can live as a member of God's family, pray for God to lead him or her to the right community. Conclude by thanking God for the time you spent together and ask Him to empower you to live lives of repentance and belief every day.

BIBLE PASSAGES FOR FURTHER STUDY

In this book we have summarized the gospel as: **the good news of who Jesus is and what Jesus has done for the glory of God and for the good of God's people.** My goal in doing so has been to provide a simple and easy-to-read summary of what the Bible says about its central message. However, my attempts at summarizing the Bible's teaching are no substitute for the words of Scripture. For this reason we have provided this collection of passages to help you dig deeper into the ideas of each of the main chapters. Though we quote entire verses below, we strongly encourage you to read these passages in your Bible in their original context. As you do, you will find even more riches on each of these topics.

INTRODUCTION
"For I [Paul] am not ashamed of the gospel, for it is the power of God for salvation to everyone who believes, to the Jew first and also to the Greek. For in it the righteousness of God is revealed from faith for faith..." (Romans 1:16-17a)

"And he [Jesus] said to them, 'Go into all the world and proclaim the gospel to the whole creation.'" (Mark 16:15)

"And you, who once were alienated and hostile in mind, doing evil deeds, he [Jesus] has now reconciled in his body of flesh by his death, in order to present you holy and blameless and above reproach before him, if indeed you continue in the faith, stable and steadfast, not shifting from the hope of the gospel that you heard, which has been proclaimed in all creation under heaven, and of which I, Paul, became a minister." (Colossians 1:21-23)

NOT WHAT WE OFTEN THINK
"I [Paul] am astonished that you are so quickly deserting him who called you in the grace of Christ and are turning to a different gospel—not that there is another one, but there are some who trouble you and want to distort the gospel of Christ. But even if we or an angel from heaven should preach to you a gospel contrary to the one we preached to you, let him be accursed. As we have said before, so now I say again: If anyone is preaching to you a gospel contrary to the one you received, let him be accursed." (Galatians 1:6-9)

"For the time is coming when people will not endure sound teaching, but having itching ears they will accumulate for themselves teachers to suit their own passions, and will turn away from listening to the truth and wander off into myths." (2 Timothy 4:3-4)

"See to it that no one takes you captive by philosophy and empty deceit, according to human tradition, according to the elemental spirits of the world, and not according to Christ." (Colossians 2:8)

THE GOOD NEWS
"I [Jesus] have said these things to you, that in me you may have peace. In the world you will have tribulation. But take heart; I have overcome the world." (John 16:33)

"The sting of death is sin, and the power of sin is the law. But thanks be to God, who gives us the victory through our Lord Jesus Christ." (1 Corinthians 15:56-57)

"(W)ho saved us and called us to a holy calling, not because of our works but because of his [God's] own purpose and grace, which he gave us in Christ Jesus before the ages began..." (2 Timothy 1:9)

"For we ourselves were once foolish, disobedient, led astray, slaves to various passions and pleasures, passing our days in malice and envy, hated by others and hating one another. But when the goodness and loving kindness of God our Savior appeared, he saved us, not because of works done by us in righteousness, but according to his own mercy, by the washing of regeneration and renewal of the Holy Spirit, whom he poured out on us richly through Jesus Christ our Savior, so that being justified by his grace we might become heirs according to the hope of eternal life." (Titus 3:3-7)

...OF WHO JESUS IS...
"He [Jesus] is the radiance of the glory of God and the exact imprint of his nature, and he upholds the universe by the word of his power..." (Hebrews 3:3)

"He [Jesus] is the image of the invisible God, the firstborn of all creation. For by him all things were created, in heaven and on earth, visible and invisible, whether thrones or dominions or rulers or authorities—all things were created through him and for him. And he is before all things, and in him all things hold together. And he is the head of the body, the church. He is the beginning, the firstborn from the dead, that in everything he might be preeminent. For in him all the fullness of God was pleased to dwell, and through him to reconcile to himself all things, whether on earth or in heaven, making peace by the blood of his cross." (Colossians 1:15-20)

"...Fear not, I [Jesus] am the first and the last, and the living one. I died, and behold I am alive forevermore, and I have the keys of Death and Hades." (Revelation 1:17-18)

"I [Jesus] and the Father are one." (John 10:30)

"Whoever has seen me has seen the Father." (John 14:9)

"In the beginning was the Word [Jesus], and the Word was with God, and the Word was God. He was in the beginning with God. All things were made through him, and without him was not any thing made that was made... And the Word became flesh and dwelt among us, and we have seen his glory, glory as of the only Son from the Father, full of grace and truth." (John 1:1-3, 14)

"For we do not have a high priest who is unable to sympathize with our weaknesses, but one who in every respect has been tempted as we are, yet without sin." (Hebrews 4:15-16)

<u>...AND WHAT JESUS HAS DONE...</u>
"You know that he [Jesus] appeared in order to take away sins, and in him there is no sin." (1 John 3:5)

"For our sake he [God] made him [Jesus] to be sin who knew no sin, so that in him we might become the righteousness of God." (2 Corinthians 5:21)

"For Christ also suffered once for sins, the righteous for the unrighteous, that he might bring us to God, being put to death in the flesh but made alive in the spirit…" (1 Peter 3:18)

"Now I would remind you, brothers, of the gospel I preached to you, which you received, in which you stand, and by which you are being saved, if you hold fast to the word I preached to you—unless you believed in vain. For I delivered to you as of first importance what I also received: that Christ died for our sins in accordance with the Scriptures, that he was buried, that he was raised on the third day in accordance with the Scriptures, and that he appeared to Cephas [Peter], then to the twelve. Then he appeared to more than five hundred brothers at one time, most of whom are still alive, though some have fallen asleep. Then he appeared to James, then to all the apostles. Last of all, as to one untimely born, he appeared also to me." (1 Corinthians 15:1-8)

"He [Jesus] disarmed the rulers and authorities [satan and his demons] and put them to open shame, by triumphing over them in him." (Colossians 2:15)

"…[A]nd what is the immeasurable greatness of his [God's] power toward us who believe, according to the working of his great might that he worked in Christ when he raised him from the dead and seated him at his right hand in the heavenly places, far above all rule and authority and power and dominion, and above every name that is named, not only in this age but also in the one to come. And he put all things under his feet and gave him as head over all things to the church…" (Ephesians 1:19-22)

"And when he [Jesus] had said these things, as they [the Apostles] were looking on, he was lifted up, and a cloud took him out of their sight. And while they were gazing into heaven as he went, behold, two men stood by them in white robes, and said, "Men of Galilee, why do you stand looking into heaven? This Jesus, who was taken up from you into heaven, will come in the same way as you saw him go into heaven." (Acts 1:9-11)

…FOR THE GLORY OF GOD…
"But now the righteousness of God has been manifested apart from the law, although the Law and the Prophets bear witness to it—the righteousness of God through faith in Jesus Christ for all who believe. For there is no distinction: for all have sinned and fall short of the glory of God, and are justified by his grace as a gift, through the redemption that is in Christ Jesus, whom God put forward as a propitiation by his blood, to be received by faith. This was to show God's righteousness, because in his divine forbearance he had passed over former sins. It was to show his righteousness at the present time, so that he might be just and the justifier of the one who has faith in Jesus." (Romans 3:21-26)

"What if God, desiring to show his wrath and to make known his power, has endured with much patience vessels of wrath prepared for destruction, in order to make known the riches of his glory for vessels of mercy, which he has prepared beforehand for glory…" (Romans 9:22-23)

"[E]ven as he [God] chose us in him before the foundation of the world, that we should be holy and blameless before him. In love he predestined us for adoption as sons through Jesus Christ, according to the purpose of his will, to the praise of his glorious grace, with which he has blessed us in the Beloved." (Ephesians 1:4-6)

"Therefore God has highly exalted him [Jesus] and bestowed on him the name that is above every name, so that at the name of Jesus every knee should bow, in heaven and on earth and under the earth, and every tongue confess that Jesus Christ is Lord, to the glory of God the Father." (Philippians 2:9-11)

...AND THE GOOD OF GOD'S PEOPLE.
"For God so loved the world, that he gave his only Son, that whoever believes in him should not perish but have eternal life. For God did not send his Son into the world to condemn the world, but in order that the world might be saved through him." (John 3:16-17)

"But he [Jesus] was pierced for our transgressions;
he was crushed for our iniquities;
upon him was the chastisement that brought us peace,
and with his wounds we are healed." (Isaiah 53:5)

"[F]or in Christ Jesus you are all sons of God, through faith." (Galatians 3:26)

"There is therefore now no condemnation for those who are in Christ Jesus. For the law of the Spirit of life has set you free in Christ Jesus from the law of sin and death." (Romans 8:1-2)

"And I [John] heard a loud voice from the throne saying, 'Behold, the dwelling place of God is with man. He will dwell with them, and they will be his people, and God himself will be with them as their God. He will wipe away every tear from their eyes, and death shall be no more, neither shall there be mourning, nor crying, nor pain anymore, for the former things have passed away.'" (Revelation 21:3-4)

"And I am sure of this, that he [God] who began a good work in you will bring it to completion at the day of Jesus Christ." (Philippians 1:6)

WHAT NOW
"He [God] has delivered us from the domain of darkness and transferred us to the kingdom of his beloved Son..." (Colossians 1:13)

"...[A]nd [Jesus was] saying, 'The time is fulfilled, and the kingdom of God is at hand; repent and believe in the gospel.'" (Mark 1:15)

"For by grace you have been saved through faith. And this is not your own doing; it is the gift of God, not a result of works, so that no one may boast. For we are his workmanship, created in Christ Jesus for good works, which God prepared beforehand, that we should walk in them." (Ephesians 2:8-10)

"In him [Jesus] you also, when you heard the word of truth, the gospel of your salvation, and believed in him, were sealed with the promised Holy Spirit, who is the guarantee of our inheritance until we acquire possession of it, to the praise of his glory." (Ephesians 1:13-14)

"And Jesus came and said to them, 'All authority in heaven and on earth has been given to me. Go therefore and make disciples of all nations, baptizing them in the name of the Father and of the Son and of the Holy Spirit, teaching them to observe all that I have commanded you. And behold, I am with you always, to the end of the age.'" (Matthew 28:18-20)

"But you are a chosen race, a royal priesthood, a holy nation, a people for his own possession, that you may proclaim the excellencies of him who called you out of darkness into his marvelous light. Once you were not a people, but now you are God's people; once you had not received mercy, but now you have received mercy." (1 Peter 2:9-10)

"And let us [Christians] consider how to stir up one another to love and good works, not neglecting to meet together, as is the habit of some, but encouraging one another, and all the more as you see the Day drawing near." (Hebrews 10:24-25)

ABOUT THE AUTHOR

Cole Brown (MABTS, MAT) has been planting and pastoring churches since 2006 following his first career in the music industry. He, his wife, and their two children currently live between Portland, Oregon and Mexico City, Mexico, where they are missionaries who work to help start and strengthen churches throughout Latin America.

He is the author of several books and also blogs for organizations such as Humble Beast, The Gospel Coalition, Witness and others.

His Spanish-language resources are available at colebrown.es.

CONCENTRATED TRUTH

Good theology is essential to good living.

Therefore, it should not be relegated to the realm of abstract theory and hard-to-read books. Good theology should be practical for daily life and accessible to everyone. This is why Cole Brown and Humble Beast together created *Concentrated Truth*.

The books in the *Concentrated Truth* series bring heavy theological concepts into our daily language and daily lives. They do so in small and easy-to-read packages aimed at transforming the way you think and live. Each book also includes a free discussion guide so you can experience such transformation in the context in which God transforms us: the Christian community.

TITLES INCLUDE:

Daddy Issues: How God Heals Wounds Caused by Absent, Abusive & Aloof Fathers

The Gospel Is...: Defining the Most Important Message in the World

Lies My Pastor Told Me: Confronting Church Clichés with the Gospel

Lies Hip Hop Told Me: Confronting Hip Hop Slogans with the Gospel

Made in United States
Orlando, FL
27 January 2023